Endorsements

I have been struggling with the relationship balance. I feel I don't have time to deal with the obligations that go along with being in a relationship. This has really let me see the different concepts others have to this. I know who I am, and I don't have to lose me if I am in a relationship. So, my singleness has been a chance for me to grow as a person, and recognize that being with me and just me is ok. I have God and am never alone. And my thoughts are not scary they are me.

Cathy Farrar

This group has me looking multi dating as an option. At first I didn't agree with it and thought it was wrong. But now I see you can use it as long as you not having sex. To see what you like and dislike.

Freddy Ray Davis

As a newlywed I am still growing out of the "independent woman" phase, and it has also bought me closer to God. I never truly "depended" on God, as much as I love him, and I had to learn that if I wasn't truly having an intimate relationship with God, how can I learn to have an intimate relationship with my husband. And your group has helped me to see that I'm not the only one that went through the things that I did when I was single, mistakes and all, but you have also helped me through confirmations to see what I need to work on to improve my relationship skills. Love you cousin and I'm proud of you.

Michelle Dickey King

Being my age, older than dirt, I have watched and read the comments of the Facebook Think Tank with the knowledge that there are intelligent single people out there who actually care about themselves and are concerned for having better dating concepts and relationships and not just dating to be a notch on someone's belt buckle of conquests. Thank you to Jennifer and all who participated in the think tank. Your future is far brighter than most singles. Amen you guys.

Susan Arthurs

TEACH ME HOW TO
LIVE *Realistically* SINGLE

Dating with Class, Character, and Integrity!

DR. JENNIFER GILBERT

TEACH ME HOW TO LIVE REALISTICALLY SINGLE DATING WITH CLASS, CHARACTER, AND INTEGRITY!

iUniverse books may be ordered through booksellers or by contacting:

iUniverse
1663 Liberty Drive
Bloomington, IN 47403
www.iuniverse.com
1-800-Authors (1-800-288-4677)

ISBN: 978-1-5320-3645-3 (sc)
ISBN: 978-1-5320-3644-6 (e)

Library of Congress Control Number: 2017916846

Print information available on the last page.

iUniverse rev. date: 12/22/2017

CARD OR SERIES TITLE PAGE

DEDICATION

I dedicate this book to all of the singles who have tried to live single according to all the rules, superficial timelines and gimmicks. We have read the books that tell us to wait 90 days for this and 3 dates for that and 10 visits before this. We have been in the churches that told us to make the lists and lay it before the Lord and believe that he will give us the desires of our hearts. We have had to endure the hardship of blind dates, speed dates, dating sites only to remain in the same situation that we were in. I honor the life that we live and I dedicate this book to those of us who want to do it right and **Realistically**.

EPIGRAPH

Dichotomy means the division into two mutually exclusive, opposed, or contradictory groups.

Let's talk about the dichotomous mindsets of singleness.

CONTENTS

FOREWORD

A few years ago a very dear friend of mine, Susan, kept telling me about friend of hers. She would tell me how this friend was going through a lot life and health issues. She would tell me about some of the problems with anxiety and panic attacks. I would describe to Susan some techniques she could tell her friend that would help when she recognized that something was happening. However, this friend needs to get to the root of problem. Search for the place where this emotional breakdown and self-doubt started. It was at that point that Susan was insistent that I meet her friend. That is when I met Jennifer Gilbert. We began to write back and forth through emails, and messaging. I finally met her in person last year at a benefit for Susan, and we have been friends since. Jennifer came to me and asked me to be on a panel of people for the research of the book you are about to read. I was honored.

Being on this panel has helped me recognize forces in my own mindsets that are hindering me from believing that I am worthy to do what I do and have a relationship. I know that sounds crazy, but during the questions I realized that I got away from the very context that I was teaching in my relationship coaching. Be yourself. This experience has brought me back to the basics. Being single is not a bad thing. It's a choice. It's not that I am bitter or angry or that I got hurt in a past relationship. It's a choice. It's a choice that God laid on my heart to do, because I forgot the one main rule. I am a spirit that has a soul and lives in a body. None of these things can I give away. So giving up my wants, my dreams, and my goals, for a relationship is not the right balance. I needed to be single in order for a work to be done in me. I also need to figure out what I want in a relationship before I jump into one. This book has helped me to remember these things. The other people that were involved in the study group, face similar issues and struggles as I do. We became a community of singles helping singles break through chains and ties that were holding us back when it comes to having a relationship based on equality and like-minded values.

I hope that whoever reads this book that God is showing you how to love yourself and understand yourself, as well as the calling he has giving you. Once you get these things, then you can have a meaningful relationship.

PREFACE

Its time out for the 90 day rules;
Time out for the celibacy blues;
Time out for telling unreal truths;
Time out for telling me to hang loose.

I need truth!
I need realism!
I need honesty!
I need candidacy!

Don't tell me what's hot!
Don't fill me with a bunch of NOTS!
Should NOT date!
Should NOT relate!
Should NOT have sex!
Should NOT reveal my best!

Keep It Real!
Keep it Honest!
Share Your Struggle!
Share Your Successes!
Share Your Failures!

Above all be **Realistic**!

*Commitments without communication
can produce a deadly situation!*

-Dr. Jennifer Gilbert

ACKNOWLEDGEMENTS

Teach Me How to Live *Realistically* Single Think Tank Group

I wish I could say that I did this work alone, but I can't. I had an amazing team of people who helped in this effort and they allowed me to pick their brains for the sake of this project. Thank you to my think tank team!

Female Members		Male Members
1.	Allene Johnson	Andre McCarty
2.	Jean Linee Casey	Brian Boyd
3.	Tarrow Henderson	Brian Dorsey
4.	Constance Pleasant	Christopher Stevens
5.	Andrea Boston	*Dexter Estes Jr.
6.	Cathy Farrar	Gary Cummings
7.	Veronica Phillips	Gregory Hughes
8.	Damaria Henderson	Jason Leonard
9.	Ava Cambric	Jourdan Flowers
10.	LaDonnia Jones	Zack Horton
11.	Rhonda Farr	Lester Adams
12.	Susan Arthurs	
13.	Pamela Hicks	

*I would like to take this moment to pay respect and dedicate this book to my good friend Dexter Estes Jr. who lost his battle to cancer before this book made it out. Gone but never forgotten!

INTRODUCTION

The beauty of dating is that it's like a buffet, you can pick and choose what you want, and you're not just stuck with a single entrée. Now just because you don't eat a dish that's available doesn't mean that it's not good because to someone else, it could be the best dish on the line.

I had a guy ask me one time how to tell a woman that he is not interested without being rude. My reply was to keep it honest and keep it real. It's not about feelings or being rude, it's about living your entire truth. I would rather someone tell me up front that I am not his cup of tea then to string me along and not honor my presence in his life, or treat me like the regret that he has within himself.

Being single for a number of years, I can attest to the fact of the current issues of dating. This book is not just for singles that have never been married, but also the ones who have been married and divorced, the ones who have even explored other options as far as relationships and dating avenues. I have had enough hang ups and the lack of progress that I made in the love arena, that I could write a separate book just for that.

This book tackles the issues that churches and dating experts may not or maybe they can't cover because they haven't lived there. For this work, I explore the various factors that may affect your life as a single and the issues that may even influence your decisions as far as the dating arena. Again, I bring you greetings from every walk of life;

✓ Raped/Virginity Taken (check)
✓ Single (Check)
✓ Married (Check)
✓ Single, while married mom (check)
✓ Divorced (check)

7

✓   Blended family (check)
✓   Married again (check)
✓   Explored alternative lifestyle (LGBT) (check)
✓   Delivered, cleansed and celibate (Check, Check, Check)
✓   Married to my career (check)
✓   Empty nest/ wild chick (check, check)
✓   Ready to settle down and marry FOREVER chick (CHECK!!!!)

In this book I plan to touch on various topics and also to categorize them to the best of my ability. As you will see in the framework, there are five basic components that affect your ability to live single, but there are several aspects that fall under those components so sit back enjoy yourself and be ready for the ride.

Living *Realistically*
Single Framework

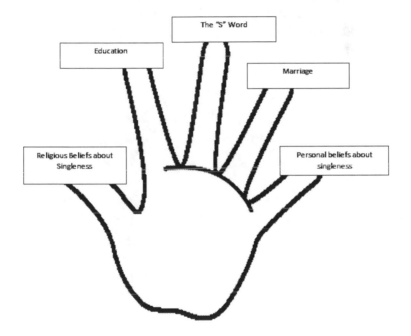

The "S" Word

Education

Marriage

Religious Beliefs about Singleness

Personal beliefs about singleness

CHAPTER 1

RELIGIOUS BELIEFS ABOUT SINGLENESS

Preface: Many of my followers are used to me writing about spiritual matters, but singleness is more than a spiritual matter, though most of the matters are spiritual in content, I want to talk Realistically and tell the common truths as well as misconceptions of this life that we live. There are a number of religious beliefs concerning singleness and living single, but the interesting thing is that many churches don't really want to talk about it, so one is left to their own devices and research of the matter.

According to Got Questions ministries, the question of a Christian staying single and what the Bible says about believers never marrying is often misunderstood.

Here are just some of the lies Satan tells us all the time.

Lie 1: You're single because you're...

You can finish the sentence yourself—just insert your adjective of choice. For me, it varies from 'fat' to 'ugly' to 'horrible' to "mean", depending on the day. But I can think of so many friends who are beautiful in the world's eyes, who are lovely, funny, kind, delightful... and single. *So many* people of all shapes, sizes and personalities are single, and people of all shapes, sizes and personalities are married. What is attractive to one may not be attractive to another. Shape, size, and personality are not why I'm single.

"God is more powerful than our social situations, our looks, our personalities, and our insecurities."

But God is more powerful than any social force or trend. The fact is that ultimately I'm single because God is in control of everything. He is sovereign. Likewise, those who are married are married because God is sovereign. Those who are widowed are widowed because God is sovereign. God is more powerful than our social situations, our looks, our personalities, and our insecurities.

Lie 2: God is not powerful enough to find you a husband!

Lie 3: You're single because God does not love you!

Lie 4: Because no-one has married you, you have no value!

Lie 5: Getting married will fix all your problems!

Lie 6: You've got to find *The One!*

Lie 7: A single person has no family!

Lie 8: It's better to marry a non-Christian than stay single for life!

Lie 9: It's too hard to be single, and you can't keep on going!

CHAPTER 2

THE EDUCATION VS. MISEDUCATION OF LIVING SINGLE

The Roots of the Word Relationship

When we look closely at the word relations hip there are a lot of roots to it such as;

Relationship-

- ➤ The state of being related or connected
- ➤ Connection by blood or marriage

Relate-

- ➤ To give an account of
- ➤ To show or have a relationship to or between; connect

Realization-

- ➤ The action of realizing

Realism

- ➤ Willingness to face facts or to give in to what is necessary

Real

- ➤ No artificial; genuine
- ➤ Not imaginary; actual

Realistic

- ➤ True to life or nature
- ➤ Ready to see things as they are and to deal with them sensibly.

Though they are all different in their own ways, the reality is that all of these words, roots and definitions play a part in the true **Realistic** beauty of a relationship. In a relationship, one must be able to relate to one another. They must be able to accept the realization that it is hard work. The realism of the matter is that every day is not going to be great, perfect, loveable or even for that matter, likeable, but in any instance, if the love is to last, it must be real. Hopefully, this book will assist in your being *Realistic* about the matter at hand and commit to making it (living *realistically* single) happen by any means necessary.

There are a lot of untruths that we have been told about the stigma of being single which is what I call "the miseducation." We already looked at the lies that the devil tells us, but what about the miseducation that is passed down from generation to generation.

Many of us as little girls were told that we were to submit and to always be under the headship of a man. While this is true to a certain extent, the sad reality is that no one ever really taught us how to be single and celebrate the beauty therein.

Being single has always been a stigmatized status and, if the truth be told, women who were single were often times frowned upon as being the harlot of the neighborhood that was after everyone's man. Even in the movies when the wife sees the single, pretty woman, the first thing she does is grab her man to ensure that it is common knowledge that he is taken. I laugh at this reaction all the time.

Now days there are over 96 million single people in the United States alone and 43% of them are over the age of 18. Sixty one percent of them have never said I do, 24% of them are divorced and 15 % are widowed.

There are a lot of what is perceived to be lonely people in the world. The truth of the matter is that more people are finding solace in their singleness and are enjoying life despite their marital status.

In 2002 there were over 904 dating services available to help the single people find each other and the companies collected $489 million that year. Today, in 2017, there are over 2500 online dating sites in the U.S. and more than 5000 worldwide raking in roughly about 2.1 billion dollars a year. Why is this important information? Because in this chapter we are about to teach you about the real logistics of being single, and the do's and don'ts of doing it right.

Education

The lack of education about being single is the root of many issues. It is much like expecting a drug addict to remain clean without giving them the tools to do so.

Not just because I am avid believer in education am I am saying this, but it is vitally important to educate yourself on the ramifications of the decisions that you make as a single person, especially if you think that you will marry or remarry, in some cases. Remember that for every action, there is a reaction or consequence and there is a rationale.

Forward Thinking No Nos!!

Action	Reaction	Rationale
Nude Pictures	I am appalled!	If they are sending me nude pics out of the blue, then how many others have the same or similar pictures?
Premarital sex	On the line	Don't get me wrong, I love sex myself, but I have also educated myself on the ramifications of it especially prior to marriage so I do my best to refrain.
Lack of dating time	I walk away feeling worthless	I will be completely transparent in saying that I am teaching you from my past errors. I have slept with men without adequate dating time and I walked away feeling worthless when it didn't pan out. I asked myself, "Was I not even worth dinner and a movie?" "Could I have done something to make it last longer?" "Why do I feel so cheap?"
Phone sex	Not happening!	Masturbation, to me, is the stem cell for the spirit of fornication. What do you mean by this? When you have phone sex, there is a greater number of spirits attached to the action than if you were to do the traditional sexual encounter. Phone sex involves the intellect, the sensuality and the five senses which mean that you have to create a false sense of intimacy and/or companionship in order for the climax to take place.

Posting on social media	CAUTION!!!	Think about the repercussions of changing your relationship status and who you are with each week. For instance, there is one guy that I know who really wanted to date me, I chose to steer clear because on his Facebook page, every other week, I saw different woman. What was to make me feel special, if he posted a picture of us together, if everyone else has already graced his page?

I'm sure there are few books out there that talk so candidly as I just did, but this is the core of what is needed if we are to learn how to live **Realistically** single, and if we want to date with class, character, and integrity.

All in all, I will always tell people to act how you want to be, and you will become the way you act. Think about it this way. Would you want nude pictures of your mate all over the world? Would you be comfortable knowing that there are a plethora of others that know their bedroom capabilities?

Being single is not rocket science, but I think it does take some forward, rational thinking. I am sure I am not telling you anything that you don't know, but I am provoking you to stop and think about the actions that you take in this dating game, especially if you desire to be in a relationship later.

Ultimately, **Realistic** dating is all about the golden rule of "Treat people like you want to be treated." If you don't want someone who has slept around, then don't sleep around. If you don't want someone who talks to a plethora of other people while talking to you, then don't you do it? All in all, if you can't take it, don't dish it out. With that being said, there is a such thing as online-dating that has become quite popular over the years and can be quite dangerous if not done correctly. Let's explore that.

Online Dating

Online Dating is the major forum these days for mingling with other singles. There are several different ways of mingling, but this method is the most prevalent, mainly for its convenience. I don't know many who have not tried, and I am sure that it is safe to say that many, if not all of us, have been burned in one way or another. THERE IS NO SAFE SITE! Paid membership or free does not guarantee security, both personally and relationally. This section is going to talk to you from my experience, as well as the experience of members from my think tank panel for this project.

What

Online dating is where you use technology, either computer or phone apps, that you post pictures and a profile of you and your desires for others to see and interact with.

Who

In online dating, we are all playing the "Who is Who" game. Many people use this forum as a way to live their "untrue life." They say they are single, and are not, they post pictures of others or of themselves, many moons ago. They are often guilty of saying what they think you want to hear, before they even know you. Especially when it comes to religion and what they think you want to hear as far as defining romance.

For women, men think that you want to hear about walking on the beach, holding hands and all, and while this may ideal for some, it gets to be pretty repetitive and often times not true in all actuality in their efforts of pursuing you in the first place. For instance, there are a number of men that I have met online that have quoted the phrase that they like to take walks in the park holding hands, they love walking on the beach and watching the sunset. They have also claimed to be romantic and want to wine and dine their woman, yet after dating them for months, I never got any of the empty promises and dreams that they stated on their profile.

When

Most people embark on the online dating experience again for the convenience. They entertain the notion for the sake of time and the fact that work, and other responsibilities that take precedence to their dating life often consume them.

Where

Dating sites can be found in many ways, in actuality it doesn't mean that you even really have to go look for it, they will come to you. There are several located in the play store app on your phone.

Why

Most people choose online dating for lack of a traditional social life. For instance, I am not a clubber, and I work a lot, so this is why online dating works best for me. Whereas my daughter has my two year old grandson, and is just not a socialite so therefore she uses the same medium.

How

How to overcome some of the obstacles;

Initial contact

I am not going to tell you some superficial, he needs to find you, because the Bible says…. Remember this is *Realistic* talk… When you meet someone online, no matter whom approaches who, do not rush to give them your number, chat a bit with them online first. Listen for any discrepancies from what they are saying, to what their profile says.

With that being said, you have to be sure to read their profiles thoroughly and make a mental note of some points on their profile, particularly the parts that concern you such as having children, wanting children, what they are looking for, whether they have a car or not. (This may seem trivial, but for some people, like me, transportation is a must.) I was in a marriage where I was the only one who drove, and the only one with a car and me playing chauffeur played out real quick. For others, it may not be an issue, but there may be something else that is a nonnegotiable like whether the person smokes or drinks, whether or not they have ever been married and things of that nature.

*__Note__-when there are discrepancies in between their profile and their conversations, oftentimes this can serve as a red flag to you. Many will say, "Oh, I just said that on my profile for this reason or for that reason," it is up to you what you let ride and not. I always count it as a red flag because it plays in trust factor for me.

Exchanging Numbers

When you exchange numbers, watch the hours that they call and the manner in which they contact you.

Red flags are;

- If there is someone who only can text and never talk, you may have to question their motive.
- If there is someone who can only talk before or after a certain time, you may have to question their motive.

These are just a few of the points that you may want to take into consideration with online dating. The number of red flags that one takes is completely a personal preference. For me, there are no more than three, before I cut communication.

Meeting Face to Face

When meeting face to face, always choose a public place for a few reasons;

- Safety is always a primary reason
- Security that you don't send the wrong signal…If you invite them to your place and vice versa, hands can move and emotions can rise and the unthinkable can happen, be it consensual or not.

I'm not saying that you walk in with that intention but you have no idea where their mind is at upon contact, nor what they have encountered on the website in the past.

Personal Rule of thumb:

I have learned to do things in threes as a rule of thumb: three chats before exchanging numbers; three conversations before a meet and greet; then a date and three dates before going any further like exchanging addresses and the rest is on you...you fill in the blanks.

!!! Caution, Caution, Caution!!!

- If they cannot adhere to your rule of thumb, be it threes or fives or even twos, USE WISDOM!
- If they are apprehensive about meeting you face to face after a specified amount of time, use caution. Or on the other hand, if they want to meet you just hours after the initial contact, that too can be a reason for concern.

Multi-dating

What is multi-dating?

Multi-dating is when a person has intentionally decided that they are not looking to date with exclusivity. This means that they are open and honest about their dating habits, desires, and aspirations. This is where the trick comes in with the "open and honest" part.

When you leave off the open and honest part, that is where the problems come in, and it sets the relationship up for failure.

When the intent to multi-date is left out, there is an inability to trust, there is a lack of communication, and the actions can be internalized as deceit, which in turn kills any opportunity or possibility for the establishment of trust for a relationship.

Multi-dating can be very tricky, let's look at the next graphic.

What should be done	What is done	The effects of non-communication
Are you okay that I talk to others while we are getting to know each other?	Just talk to others and hide it	Trust is broken
Make others aware that multi-dating does not mean multiple partners!	You leave others to their imagination	Trust is broken

What multi-dating is NOT!

The point should be made abundantly clear that multi-dating does not mean that you are sleeping with everyone. It is not a pass to activate the infamous player's card. It is not a means of being unfaithful because with multi-dating, there is a mutual understanding that there is no real exclusivity to one person until both parties agree to it.

Multi-dating is not being insensitive to another's feelings and making them feel as though they are waiting to be drafted to the team of the relationship.

The Pros and Cons of Multi-Dating

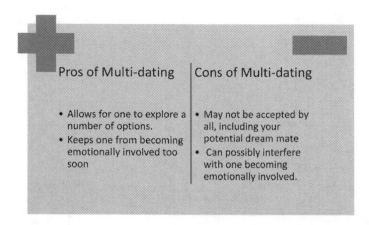

Pros of Multi-dating	Cons of Multi-dating
• Allows for one to explore a number of options. • Keeps one from becoming emotionally involved too soon	• May not be accepted by all, including your potential dream mate • Can possibly interfere with one becoming emotionally involved.

Multi-dating definitely takes a level of maturity and personal responsibility. The biggest part of the responsibility is taking everyone who's involved feelings into consideration. There is definitely a level of sensitivity that has to be implemented when giving this method of dating a try.

Soul Ties Are Real!

The complexity of relationships and singleness is a topic that is hardly, if ever, given due diligence in churches. We are always just told to save ourselves and not to sleep around. However, if you are anything like me, you need to know the rationale behind this belief. At the very root of it all are soul ties.

A soul tie is like a linkage in the soul realm between two people. It links their souls together, which can bring fourth both beneficial results and/ or negative results.

The positive effect of a soul tie: In a godly marriage, God links the two together and the Bible tells us that they become one flesh. As a result of them becoming one flesh, it binds them together and they will cleave onto one another in a unique way. The purpose of this cleaving is to build a very healthy, strong and close relationship between a man and a woman.

Matthew 19:5, "And said, For this cause shall a man leave father and mother, and shall cleave to his wife: and they twain shall be one flesh."

Soul ties can also be found in close strong or close friendships. They are not just limited to marriage, as we can see with King David and Jonathan:

1 Samuel 18:1, "And it came to pass, when he had made an end of speaking unto Saul, that the soul of Jonathan was knit with the soul of David, and Jonathan loved him as his own soul."

The negative effect of a soul tie: Soul ties can also be used for the devil's advantage. Soul ties formed from sex outside of marriage causes a person to become defiled:

Genesis 34:2-3, "And when Shechem the son of Hamor the Hivite, prince of the country, saw her, he took her, and lay with her, and defiled her. And his soul cleaved unto Dinah the daughter of Jacob, and he loved the damsel, and spoke kindly unto the damsel."

This is why it is so common for a person to still have 'feelings' towards an ex-lover that they have no right to be attracted to in that way. Even 20 years down the road, a person may still think of their first lover... even if he or she is across the country and has their own family, all because of a soul tie!

Demonic spirits can also take advantage of ungodly soul ties, and use them to transfer spirits between one person to another. I remember one young man I led through deliverance; he was facing severe demonic visitations and torment all thanks to an ungodly soul tie. I led him to break the soul tie, and the attacks stopped completely!

Ezekiel 23:17, "And the Babylonians came to her into the bed of love, and they defiled her with their whoredom, and she was polluted with them."

The Dichotomy of Singleness

The definition of dichotomy is the division of two mutually exclusive, opposed and contradictory groups. In the instance that we are speaking of we are going to look at the catch 22 of many states that singles find themselves in.

Financial Security

The dichotomy of financial security, especially from the standpoint of a woman is that the potential partner may very well feel unneeded and lack the validation that comes with the mutual financial dependence that many desire. Many men are used to the expectation of being the provider for the household. However, today, the women are leading in the job market and workforce and have learned how to hold their own. More women are becoming more successful and business oriented and even entrepreneurs, and this is where the dichotomy comes in because how does she validate the male while not "dumbing down" or demeaning her own accomplishments?

Intimacy

One of the biggest dichotomies is the issue of intimacy, especially sex though they are two very different concepts. The reason that this is a dichotomy is the fact that many of us may in all actuality want to save ourselves for marriage, but the reality of it is that we do not want our wedding night to be haunted by a bad sexual encounter. So the question becomes, "Do I save myself for marriage and hope for best?" or "Do I "test drive" the car" before I buy to ensure that it is a good "fit" for me and my desires?" Yes Christendom says, God will supply all of your needs, however, the reality is that we all need that earthly reassurance and again this is the truth that is not spoken nearly enough. Again, I am not telling you to or not to partake in premarital sex, but it is a true dichotomy that needs to be explored.

Living arrangements

To shack or not to shack, that is the question? This dichotomous topic is a hot one as well. If the man has his own place, and the woman has her own place, it is a wonderful thing, however, what happens when they decide to tie the knot, who gives up their place? Should it be the man or the woman, or both and they go and find a new mutual place together?

Professional Accomplishments

This one is near and dear to my heart. As a woman with an excessive amount of education, it is very difficult if not merely impossible to find someone of equal status who is single, faithful, committed and humble. I am often asked by men, "Do you even consider the average blue collar worker?" My response is always the same. I am open to whoever can love me honestly and earnestly, and who has morals and values to match those that I possess and seek in a mate. On the flip side of the token, many men won't even give me a shot due to my accomplishments. How would one handle this?

Child Rearing

This can be a tricky one and can be seen as a double standard by some. I was a single mom when I at one point in my life. I would only date men who had children, didn't want children or were willing to accept mine as theirs. That was years ago. Now that my children are grown and gone, I find myself not wanting to date men with small children, who want to have children, and who are not willing to accept mine for theirs, though they are not in the home. This is a dichotomy to me not so much a double standard. I feel at this point in my life, I am done raising children, especially with my career, having to spend all my days with other children, I am now at a point where I want to just enjoy life with my mate and I. I am not against us coming together as a blended family for the holidays, but as far as day in and day out, I am not really open to being with a man with small children. Perhaps your issue is not the same as mine, but the dichotomy of child rearing is still ever present.

CHAPTER 3

THE "S" WORDS

There are several S words that relate to being single and they will be addressed here. The biggest one that comes to everyone's mind is SEX. This is the taboo subject that churches shy away from, the world promotes, the body desires, but the mind can't comprehend the long term effects of.

SEX

The Effects of Sex

The one topic that everyone wants to talk about, but no one wants to embrace the reality of its impact on singleness is sex. Now there are several different approaches that we can take to this topic and we are going to explore them all. Sex is the one topic that no one will really talk about especially in the Christian "Single's ministry." As a single, I completely understand the struggle, and yes I said "STRUGGLE." Being called to ministry myself, I understand the imbalance of fleshly desires. There are a number of factors that can influence your sexual desires. There are influences such as;

- The Media
- Your own mentality
- Peer Pressure
- Past Behaviors
- Other Issues

In no way am I taking away the self-accountability that has to take place, but the reality is there is a reason that you possess your current feelings about sex. If you are looking for me to tell you that it is or is not ok to have sex, I will not do that. What I will do is tell you to move according to your convictions. I will share the causes and effects of the sexual encounter though. That alone may scare some of you straight into celibacy. See the truth of the matter is that sex is a very spiritual experience. It takes but a moment to make lifetime exchanges. Watch this;

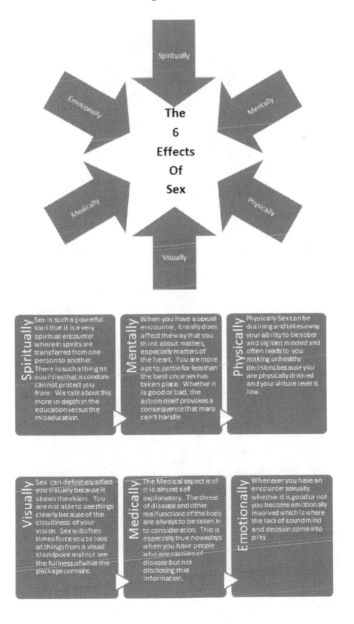

The Influences of Sex

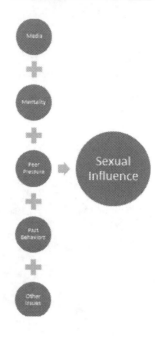

Media

The media plays a huge part in our sexual energies. Have you ever been fasting and or trying to abstain from a thing and the first thing that pops on television is your favorite restaurant with a new menu item or your favorite menu item on sale? So it is the sexual realm. I remember one time as soon as I tried to make up in my mind that I was going to abstain and remain celibate until my mate arrives, then all of sudden my "dream man" appears either on social media, a dating site or some other form of media. Of course, if it was on a dating site I had to meet him and when I did, OMG!!! He was just like I like them, tall, dark, handsome, baldheaded and smelling good. Lord have mercy! Now it didn't take long for my weariness to strengthen when I realized that he was clearly a wolf in sheep's clothing.

I sometimes struggle with the dating of today's world. I remember when dating was going out and having dinner and walks in the park and really conversing (not texting) and getting to know one another. Nowadays, its more, "Can I come over and just hold you!" Most of the time this interprets to you know what. I would be lying if I said I never fell for this trick because I have, and I would beat myself up when it occurred. But the media has created today's dating frenzy and sadly enough we fall for the bait a number of times before we learn our lesson.

Mentality

If you are constantly in the mindset of sex and that is your mental address most of the time, of course sex is going to be the driving force to many of your decisions. I wish that I could say that only men walk around with this mentality, but as a recovered sex addict myself, I digress and say that we, as a group, have a tendency to think of sex on more than a norm or more than what is needed. This is one of the reasons why I always encourage singles to guard their minds when it comes to this matter. Sex is literally a mind over matter element to our being. Yes, it is a natural craving, but it is also one that can be restrained if you want to be.

Peer Pressure

As much as many of us may not want to admit it, even as adults, we all fall prey to the infamous "peer pressures" of life. I have one friend who has dinner with his homeboys every Sunday and I am certain that within their conversation, whether they want to admit it or not, the conversation of sex creeps into the gathering. So it is with my friends and I. I, for one, know my limitations so I cannot talk about the subject for too long without feeling some type of way so therefore, I try to keep my conversations about it to a minimum. With that being said though, within those conversations that you have with your friends, you cannot convince me that, if they said they tried something new or different and they spoke highly of its effect, I am not convinced that you, yourself would not want to try it or something like it. Be it a position, a location, a product, an intimate idea, whatever the case, we call compare notes, tips and tricks at one point or another which is all a form of peer pressure.

Past Behaviors

Many of us have had past behaviors that influence our sex lives such as rapes, molestations, promiscuity and the like. Yes, you are no longer a victim to the act, we claim your healing, however, and you can still be affected by the event. Being a victim of rape and molestation for a number of years, it lead to me being promiscuous, which in turn led me to suffer with a sex addiction that I claim healing from today, however, if I don't guard my mind and my imagination, I can relapse at any time. This is the manner in which my past behaviors influence my sex life. If you remember in the beginning of the book, I told you that I can relate to you on many different levels;

Again, I bring you greetings from every walk of life;

✓ Raped/Virginity Taken (check)
✓ Single (Check)
✓ Married (Check)
✓ Single, while married mom (check)
✓ Divorced (check)
✓ Blended family (check)
✓ Married again (check)
✓ Explored alternative lifestyle (LGBT) (check)
✓ Delivered, cleansed and celibate (Check, Check, Check)
✓ Married to my career (check)
✓ Empty nest/ wild chick (check, check)
✓ Ready to settle down and marry FOREVER chick (CHECK!!!!)

All of these elements of my being have an effect on my beliefs and performances when it comes to sex. It is not often that you see a woman so open to sharing about her sex addiction and the behaviors that lead to the diagnoses, but I am that woman that is secure enough in my present to share my past in hopes of helping someone else's future be better than it could have been.

Other Issues

Many people walk around with the belief that perhaps if I had mate, then I would not have to masturbate! Masturbation is the stem cell to the sin of fornication. Your mentality has a large part to do with your investment in the weight of sex. If you constantly think about it, if you are one of those who feel like you have to have it, so shall your actions be. When I was at the climax of my addiction, I couldn't think of anything else but sex, it was literally the driving force to all of my decisions. I had to take control of my thoughts. Yes, I prayed and asked for God's assistance, but at the end of the day the responsibility still lied in the palms of my hands.

Settling

There is no room for settling when *Realistically* dating. There are a number of reasons why people choose to settle for less than healthy relationships and we are going to explore a few, probably the most popular. But before we do that, let's explore the meaning of settling.

To "settle for" means to be satisfied with. To be "satisfied with" means to fulfill the desires, expectations, needs, or demands of (a person, the mind, etc.); give full contentment to. To be "content" means to be satisfied with what one is or has; not wanting more or anything else. None of these equate to happiness, nor are they healthy to the whole person.

I believe there are four elements to your state of singleness and all of them must be explored in order to attain what is your heart's desire or even to know what your desire is. Those four elements are the needs, desires, aspirations and beliefs.

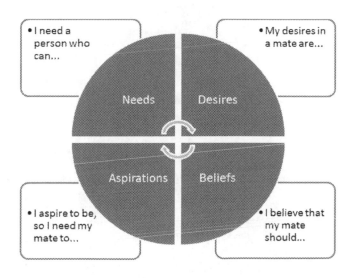

- I need a person who can...
- My desires in a mate are...

Needs   Desires

Aspirations   Beliefs

- I aspire to be, so I need my mate to...
- I believe that my mate should...

<u>Needs</u>

The first of the four elements of singleness is the "Need." Under our personal beliefs come the maturity to discern what you "need" and what you "want." There is a very distinct difference in what one needs versus what one wants. One may need a spouse who can cook because they can't perform the task. On the other hand, another may want a spouse who can cook, not because they can't, but because they don't like to.

Needs are defined as

- ➢ something that must be done; obligation
- ➢ a lack of something necessary, useful or desired
- ➢ to suffer from the lack of something important to life or health
- ➢ to be necessary
- ➢ to be without; require

The focus remains on the last three definitions provided by Webster's Elementary Dictionary. The revelation of a need in regards to a relationship is those things that are important to your life, health and survival. This understanding comes not only with revelation, but also with a language change. For example, I was always one to say, "I need a man who works!" The reality of it is that what I REALLY need is a man with financial assets to bring to our table of contribution.

The reason for this language change is that you are limiting your blessing. What if God wants you to have a mate who is retired or financially wealthy, where he doesn't necessarily have to work, but can contribute financially to the household or better yet, can completely finance the household?

Some people may say that to have a mate who works is not a NEED because they are financially able to care for the household on their income alone.

While this may be true, the truth of the matter is that this agreement could be potentially dangerous for the stability of the relationship. What if, God forbid, something happens to you or to your health, the *Realistic* desire is that you need someone who can pick up the slack and gather the pieces to keep the household afloat until you are back on your feet. A little later in this experience we are going to explore "flame killers" of which finances, can are often are one of those elements that can and will kill every relationship to some capacity. This is another support to the claim that a mate with a financial contribution is a NEED not a Desire.

Desires

The second of the four elements are the "Desires" of an individual. Desires are those things that we dream of in a mate, but the reality is that we won't die, nor will it be a deal breaker if the person does not possess these qualities. For instance, I am only 5'2' and I really like tall men, I haven't dated many, however, they make me feel safe and guarded, but if I meet another man that is 5'2', God forbid, I won't disregard him because of it.

Desires are defined as;

> ➢ a longing or craving, as for something that brings satisfaction or enjoyment:
> ➢ A desire for fame.
> ➢ An expressed wish; request.
> ➢ Something desired.
> ➢ Sexual appetite or a sexual urge.

I desire a man who can cook, just because it would be great to come home to a home cooked meal at times or be served breakfast in bed. Will I die if I don't find someone to meet this desire? NO! However, it is just an added bonus.

Aspirations

Aspirations are defined as;

> ➢ A strong desire, or aim; ambition
> ➢ A goal or objective that is strongly desired

The third of the four elements of singleness is aspirations and this is a very heavy topic that we must take our time to explore. Oftentimes, we as singles seek after people who are good for us in our "right now." We forsake the goals and aspirations that we have for our future and then we find ourselves unhappy when one of two things happen;

> ➢ the "right now" mate is complacent where we are and not willing to aspire with y0u to help you reach those goals, or
> ➢ You reach those goals (aspirations for yourself) against all odds and then the relationship suffers because, you two have grown apart.

I used to not believe in the fact that people can grow apart until I experienced it myself. Due to me being a teen mom, I didn't attend college until later. I had talked to my then husband about me wanting to attend college and what my career track aspirations were. He was completely on board and all for it, in full support. When I finished my associates at the local college, we had to move to a bigger city for me to continue school. He didn't want to move because he was complacent where we were. I had to make the hard decision of choosing my husband or my aspirations. I chose my aspirations. This was a direct reflection of a poor choice made in choosing my "Mr. Right Now" vs my "Mr. Right." We clearly grew apart. I wanted more out of life and he told me he did too but when it came time for the rubber to meet the road he wanted to sit on the side lines. It was a very hard decision and there were many other factors that I had to take into consideration but given the same choice. I wouldn't change a thing.

Beliefs

The last of the four elements of singleness is Beliefs.

Beliefs are defined as;

> ➢ something believed, an opinion or conviction
> ➢ confidence in the truth or existence of something not immediately susceptible to rigorous proof
> ➢ confidence; faith; trust

When I say the word "beliefs" most people automatically think religion. Though this is one element of beliefs, there are so many other elements that fall under this same category and are just as critical to the success or the demise of the relationship. These are what I call "Flame Killers"

Flame Killers

In every relationship there is what I call "flame killers" that will kill the flame of any relationship no matter what the status. Those elements are;

- ❖ Sex
- ❖ Deceit
- ❖ Money
- ❖ Communication
- ❖ Outside commitments

Flame killers are those underlying issues (beliefs) that every relationship has that soon become the underlying issue of every problem. Have you ever had a senseless argument that got super-heated and you never knew why? What happened? How did we get this out of that? Where did that come from? When you get to the core of it 100% of the time one of the flame killers are to blame. I'm going to share the major categories, but in the next graphic you will see the subcategories that fall under them.

Flame killers are the targets that most therapists try to get to, but no one wants to talk about. They are the issues of life that churches try to get you delivered from. They tell the truth of how much a matter (belief) really means to you and how much you have been effected by a thing, be it from your past, present, or future.

You have to watch out because flame killers will find their way into your bedroom, and will feel like an artic igloo between you and your mate that no one wants to chisel at for fear of a combustible explosion.

So what happens is we shovel manure on top of it and act as though it doesn't bother us when in reality it stays at the forefront of our minds at all times and so whatever that issue is, it manifests itself in several different ways.

We are about to explore the five major categories and see how they manifest within the relationship.

The Root Causes and Their Explanations

Sex	Deceit	Money	Communication	Outside Commitment
•too much of it expected • Not enough of it received •boring •unsatisfactory	•Telling lies •conversations carried outside of the room with no explanation •a seperate life lead by another •Cheating	•Not enough of it •Imbalance of income •no agreement on the use of it	•lines of communication crossed •lack of communication •no clear expecation of communication •too much communication (yes you can have too much)	•Family expectations •Careers •Jobs •Religion

How many arguments can you think of that when you really sat down at the end of the day and was completely honest with yourself, you can say that these roots were not the actual cause of it? Maybe not all of them, but for sure one or two of them are. Let's be real about it, when we are sexually frustrated, everything seems to get under our skin. When we have been deceived in one way or another, we walk through life with an eyebrow up at every little incident that occurs. When money is the issue, we fuss and fight about it because we feel there has to be a better way to handle matters to ensure that ends are being met. Communication is one of the greatest flame killers because it is the source of everything. Think about it. Your sexually frustrated, your mate says, "Why didn't you just say something" Your mate cheats on you (deceit), you ask, "Why didn't you just come and talk to me and tell me what you needed before you did that?" Money is mysteriously missing from the budget or the household and your spouse says what? "Why didn't you just tell me?" You have a family engagement or function to attend, you and your spouse are double booked to go in different directions and what is the first thing that they say, "If you would have told me…!" What am I saying? Communication is the threshold of every relationship, so no wonder it is the most critical component that is always attacked. The devil knows if he can keep you from communicating, it will never work.

Understanding these elements or what are affectionately known as "flame killers" are the foundational forces to every relationship which means whenever or however you choose to enter into a relationship, these components must be protected from the plague of disaster by establishing them and nurturing them from the gate or the onset of the relationship.

I am hoping that after taking this long walk around the topic of settling that you will see how important it is that we don't do it. What happens is that you settle for one thing and you don't think of the attachments that come with that settlement. Settling for something that was on your "needed" list can be a detriment to you, and could be potentially dangerous and life threatening. Using the same example that we did in that chapter about having someone who is able to make regular financial contributions to the household, we will explore the detriment of settling.

You say, "I need someone who makes regular financial contributions to the household," but you settle for less. There are other issues that are attached to that which you settled for by proxy meaning, you did not look at the package deal.

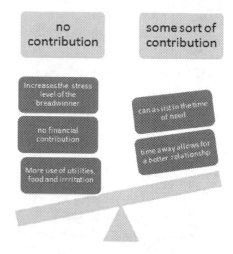

As you see, the balance is leaning toward the weight of the liability that has entered into your life. Many people choose to buy into the miserable Betty Wright mentality that says, "A piece of a mate is better than no

mate at all." This is not healthy, *Realistic*, or true. This leans more into the chapter that deals with the education versus the miseducation that we already talked about. When you settle it does more harm to you than good. Let's look at some of the reasons that people settle for less than healthy relationships.

All in all settling does more harm than good to both you and your potential mate so don't do it.

Safety

Safety is an S word that this book would not be complete if we didn't explore it. As we talked about online dating, we mentioned some of the elements of safety when it comes to meeting and greeting and sharing information. However there is also an element of safety that comes when you are considering or are even in a relationship. In my counseling sessions, I always share these "Share the 8 Before It's Too Late" definitions. Below are the eight mental and emotional signs of domestic abuse used by one person to gain power and control over another? These are some behaviors that you should look for or at least be aware of when entertaining the idea of a relationship with someone.

1. Intensity

Someone you just met exhibits the following behavior: LYING or exaggerating; INSISTING you move in/get married/have kids immediately; trying to win over friends and family; OVER THE TOP gestures like expensive gifts/dates, extreme love letters; sweeping you off your feet; BOMABARDING you with texts and emails; behaving obsessively and non-stop calls.

How you start a thing is a good indication of how it will continue. Many confuse intensity and attention and while they are synonymous, they are very different levels of severity.

2. Jealousy

Behaving IRRATIONALLY when you get a promotion, job or new friend, becoming ANGRY when you speak to the opposite sex, persistently ACCUSING you of cheating, resenting your time with friends, family, coworkers and activities, DEMANDING to know private details of your life.

This is pretty much self-explanatory. This is another reason to keep your exchange of information brief and subtle, don't give too much information too fast. The demand for more information should be a red flag for anyone.

3. Control

TELLING you how to dress, when to speak and what to think, showing up UNINVITED to your home, school, or job, CHECKING your cell phone, emails, Facebook, going through your belongings, timing/FOLLOWING you, monitoring spending/WITHHOLDING money, sexually coercing you.

Oftentimes this behavior is covered with the words, "I am just looking out for you and want to make sure that you are okay!" You have to pay attention to intentions and motives. Use your discernment/intuition as a guiding force. If it doesn't feel right, it probably isn't.

4. Isolation

INSISTING you only spend time with them, making you emotionally, psychologically or financially DEPENDENT, preventing you from seeing your friends, family, or children, FORBIDDING you from going anywhere or speaking to anyone, keeping you home.

Caution is a must in this aspect. Keywords such as, "I want you all to myself!" is a HUGE red flag and you should run immediately.

5. Criticism

Calling you overweight, UGLY, STUPID, or crazy, ridiculing your beliefs, ambitions or friends, claiming, they're the only one who really cares about you, making you feel bad about yourself, BRAINWASHING you to feel worthless, accusing you of being a bad parent.

Criticism is one of the worst, but most often used, especially for successful mates who are "more accomplished" than their counterparts. Even by saying, "Just because I don't have...like you, doesn't make me any less than you!" Is a subtle put down enveloped in insecurity? Use caution!

6. Sabotage

Making you MISS work or school by starting a fight or having a MELTDOWN, being needy when you're busy or doing well, making you believe your crazy, alone, or helpless, HIDING your money, keys or phone, stealing your belongings, DESTROYING your self-esteem.

Gas lighting is the term that comes to mind when I read this. Gas lighting is a form of sabotage and means that people will play with your mind to try to alter your reality they will cause you to doubt your sanity through the use of psychological manipulation. They say things like,

"You're Crazy that never happened!"

"I never said that!"

"You must be confused again!"

"That's not right, you're remembering things wrong!"

"What are you talking about?"

This happens when you know without the shadow of a doubt that you know a thing or that a thing happened and they try to make you think that you are crazy and make you doubt yourself.

7. Blame

Making you feel GUILTY and responsible for their aggressive or DESTRUCTIVE behavior, blaming the world or you for their PROBLEMS, threatening SUICIDE/self-harm because of something that you did/you want to leave, always saying, "This is your FAULT" or "You made me do this."

This should definitely never happen in a dating/courting relationship. If it ever gets this deep RUN!!!

8. Anger

OVERREACTING to small problems, frequently losing control, violent OUTBURSTS, having severe mood swings, drinking or partying when upset, THREATENING to hurt you or loved ones, picking FIGHTS, having a history of violent behavior and making you feel AFRAID.

This is another instance where you should RUN!!!

Now that we have looked at the eight individual attributes, let's now look at the overview of a healthy vs. unhealthy relationship. This is the time to really evaluate if you are in an abusive relationship or not and take the necessary steps needed to acknowledge it and take action.

Healthy versus Unhealthy Relationships

Healthy relationships are all about togetherness and making both parties feel as though they are joint heirs to the kingdom that is the relationship. No one is more important or more valuable than another and all interests are shared amongst both parties.

There are many types of abuse but they all fall under the 4 major types of abuse which are sexual, physical, neglect, and emotional. Emotional abuse is one of the worst but most prevalent types of abuse. Above we talked about some red flags but now let's explore some of the methodologies of the emotional abuser. Some parts are the same and some are not.

Signs of Emotional Abuse

SIGNS OF EMOTIONAL ABUSE

THE EMOTIONAL ABUSER:

- humiliates you, either alone or in front of other people.

- calls you "too sensitive" when you respond to abusive comments.

- belittles you and trivializes your hopes, dreams and accomplishments.

- tries to control you and your behavior.

- isolates you from family and friends.

- blames you for his or her problems.

- gaslights you to make you doubt your sanity.

- has extra-marital affairs, becomes emotionally distant or withholds sex to control you.

- lacks respect and points out your mistakes or shortcomings.

We can all look at this list and say, "No way, this will never happen to me!" but the truth of the matter is that it happens all the time. this is the most common form of abuse because it doesn't leave any outside bruises or evidence but it is also the reason why many of us have issues in future relationships because we have fallen victim to the abuse from prior relationships and have not fully healed as of yet.

Whatever you do don't ever think that abuse is a one-time occurrence. The reality is that it never happens one time; it is a vicious cycle that repeats itself.

Cycle of Violence

Tension Building
Batterer increases anger, threats or controlling behavior
Tension increases
Victim feels like they have to "walk on eggshells"
Victim feels the need to keep batterer calm
Poor communication
Incidents of abuse may begin

Calm Phase
Batterer acts like abuse did not happen
Abuse may be absent
Victim feels abuse is over and batterer has changed
Note: The cycle of abuse may take hours, weeks, months, or years. In most cases, the calm phase will grow shorter in length.

Cycle of Violence

Crisis Phase
Batterer is highly unpredictable
Batterer claims s/he is "losing control"
Victim feels helpless and trapped
Batterer is emotionally, physically, or sexually abusive
Victim is traumatized
Batterer blames victim

Make-Up/Honeymoon Phase
Batterer is loving, apologetic and attentive to victim
Batterer may buy gifts for the victim
Batterer may promise to change or it will never happen again
Batterer may blame the victim for causing the abuse
Victim feels guilty and responsible
Victim minimizes abuse

Being in an abusive relationship myself a time or two, I have become very aware of the signs, signals and cycles of it. Just when you think it's over and things are better than ever, it happens again. Pay close attention to this cycle because I promise you it can save your life. Why am I putting all of this in a single's book? Because this is the time when you can make the decision as to what you will and will not put up with. This is also the time when you can look for the signs and signals and can make a conscious decision to free yourself before it's too late.

<u>Singleness</u>

There are several different definitions of singleness nowadays. Unfortunately, it's no longer just a matter of married or unmarried. There is also singleness as in unmarried: ready to date, unmarried: not interested in dating as well as:

- Seeking Long term
- Looking to Dating

- Looking for Friends
- I want to get Married
- Living Together
- Divorced
- Widowed
- Separated
- Looking for casual dating no commitment
- Want to date but nothing serious
- I want a relationship
- Serious and looking

This is why it is important to make sure you explicitly ask the questions that you want to know, "Are you single?" don't cut it no more, and you can't assume that they are single because they are on a single's dating site or at a single's event or function, many married people attend these events as well.

There is another aspect of singleness that I want to explore and that is the singleness of mind, body, soul and spirit. When we are involved in relationships in any capacity, we give of ourselves to others and have a tendency to neglect ourselves. During our time of singleness, it is important that we collect ourselves and our member back from the people who were unworthy of receiving them. The people who took advantage of us and never deposited back into us anything near the amount of withdrawals that they made. This is the time to recover all.

We cannot expect them to deposit or return to us all that we invested, so it is up to us to reclaim ourselves and ask God to redeem the hands of time. It is a time for us to pour back into ourselves the energy that we have poured into others over time.

When we really look at it, singleness is not just a status but a state of mind and a way of life, a lifestyle if you would. Only when we become single, can God really breathe upon our efforts of finding a mate. Gathering our member is metaphorical for regaining control of our lives and our being, purifying ourselves of the issues that have plagued us in days gone by.

Then and only then can we experience the satisfaction that we are about to learn about.

Satisfaction

Satisfaction comes in finding a peace in the situation that we find ourselves in. Singleness, contrary to popular belief, is not a curse, but can really be a blessing especially to those who have found themselves in number of failed relationships. Especially if you are like the masses that get into a relationship and lose yourself, you need time to become satisfied with being alone.

This is the time to come to peace and terms with the reason or reasons why things happened the way that they did. Not only that, but in your reflection of what happened, you are thinking in a forward fashion that says, "I can't do anything about what happened then, but how can I pick up the pieces to ensure that it doesn't happen again." It is not by accident that these S words are divinely aligned the way that they are. When you find yourself single, for whatever reason, you have to first become satisfied, and/or content with the state that you are in before you can proceed on to self-solidarity. It is a process that cannot skip a step or there will be consequences to pay that may not be worth the cost.

Singleness	Satisfaction	Self-Solidarity
The state that one finds themselves in when a relationship ends.	The condition that one has to discover, despite the feelings that they may experience after the loss.	The place of purity and wholeness that one should reside in before trying to enter into another relationship after closure has taken place.

Self-Solidarity

This is a term that I coined to be defined as a time when there is a union and a fellowship arising within one's self that creates a union of all elements of your being to include, feelings, purpose, interest, mistakes, emotions and responsibilities.

This is the time that one takes to become completely in tune **with** themselves and their own personal needs and desires **for** themselves before they deflect it on to another. See oftentimes what happens is that we leave one relationship and enter into another to fill a void that was created by the loss of the last relationship. The issue with this is that we have a tendency of taking the issues of one relationship into another one. This behavior causes for us to see a reflection of our past in our present and soon to be future endeavors as far as relationships are concerned.

In the chart below I have named the six elements of self. These are the elements that must be aligned in order for one to present their whole healthy self into a new relationship.

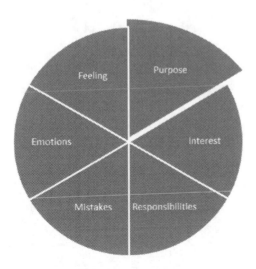

Let's look at each element individually before we dive into the meat and potatoes of this section.

Feelings

-a temporary reaction to an occurrence, lasts for a short period of time, but can trigger some irrational behaviors if not restrained.

Emotions

-stronger than feelings, but are attached to the feelings, and can take those feelings to a degree that can have lasting effects. Left unaddressed, they can definitely lead to irrational behaviors.

Purpose

-purpose is all about realigning yourself with the God given purpose that he intended for you. Another element of purpose is discovering what his purpose was for that relationship. We know that all things do work together for our good, even when they don't feel good or look good at the time.

Interest

-You definitely want to take the time to re-explore your interests and maybe even rediscover or discover some new ones after the encounter that you just experienced.

Mistakes

-This is the time that you take to reflect on the mistakes that you made especially when it comes to the demise of the relationship, seeing what part you played in it and how NOT to make the same mistakes which leads us to the final element.

Responsibilities

-Taking responsibility for your actions is a major part of the self-solidarity. When you take responsibility, you hold yourself accountable as well as others that may come in your future endeavors.

Now let's see how this all plays out in your living *Realistically* single.

We all have our levels of issues, that goes without saying. The problem lends itself to the fact of whether we have dealt with the issues or not. I use what I call the "Accessory Model."

The accessory model exemplifies the fact that we all have accessories called "experiences" in the lane of love. Some of us have had head on collisions, and others have just had mere fender benders. Whatever the case, the experiences have to be addressed and partitioned in a manner that is healthy and productive and can be retrieved for the sake of reference, not reverence. What do I mean? Let's see…

Reference (+)

Reference →

- referred to as a "mention" without an emotional connection
- used as a learning tool and mentioned in a "by the way" type manner
- placed neatly in the mind to keep from making the same mistake again or ignoring unhealthy behaviors in one's self and/or in others.

Reverence (-)

- a deep respect and emotional connection to the pain
- used as a crutch that is mentioned from the "victim" standpoint
- mentioned with details and in the midst of a long discussion to include, "she said…. she said…"

Reverence →

<u>The Accessory Model</u>

Let's dig even deeper into the accessory model…

Briefcase
- Your organized experiences are used as learning tools

Luggage
- Your learning tool kit that has been addressed and organized, yet are very diverse

Baggage
- Open wounds that are unaddressed, unorganized, nonproductive, yet manageable.

Overage
- Open wounds that are unaddressed, unorganized, nonproductive nonmanageable, hard to detect due to clutter, therefore hard to address and are overwhelming.

Briefcase

Your organized experiences used as learning tools

The briefcase is what we all long to have. It is small, organized and tools can be retrieved relatively easily. During conversations such as Q & A sessions with a potential mate, experiences are shared as requested and the responses are brief and to the point.

The briefcase represents the mind of the individual. Issues are neatly compartmentalized and ready for easy retrieval upon request.

Briefcase Conversation

Q. For example, the potential mate asks, "What are you looking for?

A. Your briefcase response is, "I am looking for my lifelong mate to spend the rest of my life with.

Q. Have you ever been married before?

A. Yes, twice, **and** I am completely divorced and I am ready to move on and you?

Luggage

Your learning tool kit is comprised of experiences that are addressed and organized, yet very diverse.

The luggage is not a negative, but it's very close to it if used incorrectly. It's almost like standing close to the curb teeter tottering there while traffic is headed in your direction. You are safe, but still at risk for danger if the wrong move is made.

The luggage mentality is still brief and organized, but there is a level of elaboration that comes with it which is where the problems can come in. The elaboration is great and may be appreciated, especially if they ask you to explain, but it's all in how you explain it that can make the difference.

Luggage Conversation

Q. For example, the potential mate asks, "What are you looking for?

A. Your luggage response is, "I am looking for my lifelong mate to spend the rest of my life with in marriage.

Q. Have you ever been married before?

A. Yes, twice, **but** I am completely divorced and I am ready to move on, because this single stuff is just not for me?

What's wrong?

TOO MUCH! It came off a little desperatish (if that be a word). It could have come off as just clarifying, but to the wrong person, it could have come off a little pushy. The responses were pretty much the same, but can you see how they could have easily turned another direction and been on the team too much level that we are about to explore.

<u>Baggage</u>

Open wounds that are unaddressed, unorganized, nonproductive, yet manageable.

The baggage is not healthy at all and is often the phase that many are in when they are fresh out of a relationship. You have just gathered your things and left. There has been no real processing, your mind, feelings, and emotions are everywhere. You are going back and forth with what they did to you and not really looking at the responsibility or accountability phase of what part you played in the matter. You are not necessarily interested in a person, you are more interested in being "saved" by someone whom you think is better. It is easy for you to come off as desperate, needy, angry and unforgiving. Watch!

Luggage Conversation

Q. For example, the potential mate asks, "What are you looking for?

A. Your luggage response is, "I am looking for my a man to spend the rest of my life with cuz I am tired of being alone. I ain't looking for no one to take care of me and I ain't looking to take care of nobody. Everyone need to pay their own way in my next relationship.

Q. Have you ever been married before?

A. Yes, twice, and I swear, I married the same person twice in a different body, both of them lazy and don't wanna work and I had to take care of everybody and everything like I was the man.

What's Wrong?

WAY TOO MUCH! This crazy person has victimized themselves and their past partners. Not only do they look desperate, but they also look enabling and their responses scream "NO CLOSURE!!!" Sad to say that this is where most people are when they leave one relationship and head to another and the first thing that the person that they are talking to may do is market on what he/she lacked and respond with, "Well I do work!" They have already won over the baggage and adopted a new problem.

<u>Overage</u>

Open wounds that are unaddressed, unorganized, nonproductive, non-manageable, hard to detect due to clutter, therefore hard to address and are overwhelming.

Overage is just that, over the top! They have stayed in the baggage state and went from relationship to relationship with the same baggage mentality and now their issues have become so plentiful that they can no longer fit it in a suitcase they need a whole treasure chest. The only issue is that on the outside, they appear to have it all together in this beautiful package, but when one opens up the "treasure chest" they see and experience trash. Old issues that have never been dealt with, feelings that have festered into the emotions of the individual. Oftentimes these people feel as though their only purpose in life is to be miserable and unhappy in love. They have become disinterested in the health of the relationship and just went into survival mode and often times will be the ones to settle for great sex, even if it's not so great, just so that they don't have to be alone. Watch how horrible this conversation goes:

Overage Conversation

Q. For example, the potential mate asks, "What are you looking for?

A. Your overage response is, "I am looking for my mate cuz I am tired of being alone. I ain't looking for no one to take care of me and I ain't looking to take care of nobody. Everyone need to pay their own way in my next relationship. I need a bae in public and a freak in the sheets. You know what I am saying, someone who can put it down and hold me down. I hope they don't have no kids cuz I am done with that and ain't trying to have no more. I want it to be just me and them.

Q. Have you ever been married before?

A. Yes, twice, and I swear, I married the same person twice in a different body, both of them lazy and don't wanna work and I had to take care of everybody and everything like I was the man. I ain't doing that no more. I need them to cook and clean, they need good credit, a car, they own place, I don't need no mama's baby, I need a whole person who is on they grown folk status, I mean they got a job, car, place, friends, great sex drive etc. You feel me?

What's Wrong?

I don't even think I need to say what all is wrong with this conversation. LOL but seriously, but how many of us have had these type of conversations? Where you have basically recapped your entire experience on dating as a whole. You nearly didn't even answer the questions because it was hidden under the junk of your issues.

So what is the solution?

DOWNSIZE!

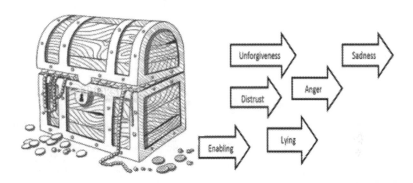

Notice how little the number of arrows is but the issues that fall within these arrows are plentiful and they are the roots of a plethora of other emotions. These are the things that you need to release before even thinking of entering into another relationship.

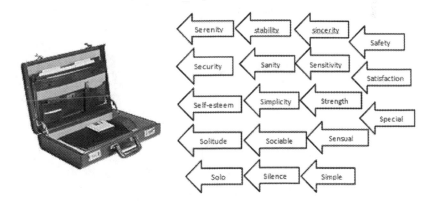

Here are all of the positive compartmentalized attributes that you need to place inside of your briefcase. These are the S words that need to become a part of your daily affirmation and devotional. These are the S words that you need to look for as well as exhibit in and of yourself.

CHAPTER 4

MARRIAGE I DO VS. I CHOOSE NOT TO

Some people view marriage as the be all and end all when in reality it is both the beginning and the end. When we as singles encounter an individual who is married in any capacity, we have to be respectful of that covenant.

In this book, I have tried to stress over and over that when **Realistically** dating with character, integrity and class, it is all about treating people how we want to be treated. If there is someone that is still in covenant with someone, that is the first line of walking away. It doesn't matter if they are separated and living in the same house or not, if there are no papers, then they are still in covenant and I have no choice but to respect that and walk away.

My rationale behind this is numerous. My thinking is;

- If they will entertain me while married to their mate, they will do the same to me.
- If I was their mate, I would want no one to come between my mate and I because who knows what can happen.
- Because of the God that I serve, who I know can reconcile anything, I like to give him the opportunity to do so in the relationships of others, because I know he can and will turn it around.

Again these are just a few of my own convictions concerning the matter. Many may ask me why I am talking about marriage in a single's book. Here is the answer to that question. Many of us date with a purpose and that purpose is to pursue the relationship through marriage. The beauty of singleness and dating is that this is the time that you can pick and choose what it is that you want and don't want. This is also the time for you to reflect and decide whether or not marriage is something that you want or not. This is the time for you to think about what you want and don't want and what you will accept and what is unacceptable. This is the time for you to ask yourself the real questions and explore the real truths about yourself, especially if you have been married before. You definitely want to take the time to see what part you played in the demise of your prior marriage(s) to ensure that it doesn't happen again.

After marriage is where the 20/20 vision comes in at and you really can make the changes that you need to make when you are single because the marriage covenant is not to be entered into lightly. You also want to be able to show your own growth and the work that you have put into yourself to your potential mate.

There are a lot of myths about marriage and relationship that have deceived us for years that I would like to explore as we encounter this chapter.

There is no such thing as a Soul Mate!

There is no such thing as a soul mate. This is a Greek myth. This is a fallacy that has been believed and passed down from generation to generation. What the real truth is that back in the Greek days, humans had double the limbs and capacities that we have now and they were connected. In a jealous rage, Zeus (A Greek god) became angry and cut the people in half and sent one half to one side of the earth and the other to the other side of the earth and these people spent their lives trying to find their "soul mate."

Another reality in this matter is that when you say that you seek your soul mate, you imply that the work of God is incomplete and imperfect which we all know is not true.

There is no such thing as your "better half"

This is another term that we have all encountered and learned as a pass down from many generations. When we really stop to think about the whole connotation of the words "better half" again it implies that we are created as incomplete beings. Nowhere in scripture is this clause verified by scripture. When we look at the story of Adam and Eve, Adam was a whole and complete person when Eve was created from his rib. When Eve was created, she too was a whole and complete being.

Another subliminal purpose of this book is to assist you in being a WHOLE and not a half. Implying that we are a "better half" says that we are not complete without our mate, which is where the stigma of dependency is rooted from.

In this book we want to assist you in how to become a whole, before entering into the covenant of marriage. This is critical because if you go in thinking that you are a half and incomplete, then that is what you will encounter on your quest to find love.

There are a lot of questions for exploration that one should ask themselves before trying to entertain the idea of marriage to someone else. I believe that the more you know about yourself prior to a relationship, the less likely you are to settle for what you don't need or desire.

Ask yourself these questions and see why the answers are so important.

Desiring Questions of Deep Self Exploration and Desire

Questions	Why it's important to know
Do I think that I want to marry or not?	This question is important because it is REALISTIC, especially when you follow up the question with "Why." Asking yourself this question keeps in perspective your desire for your life and also speaks to your motive for your action.
What do I want to be career wise?	This is important because it can affect the type of mate that you may need or desire. For instance, if you are a world traveler with your career, a clingy person that needs you home every night may not be the best fit for you. This is where thinking forward comes into play.
Am I one who needs consistent companionship?	This question kind of plays into the last one. If you are one who needs consistent companionship as in one who is home every night, a truck driving mate, may not be your best choice or someone with any sort of demanding career.
What do I need emotionally?	This question plays into the self-solidarity piece. Becoming aware of your emotional state as well as your emotional needs. BE HONEST and

	Realistic about this matter because it will manifest itself in your relationship later on.
What do I need spiritually?	One of the questions that I asked the think tankers is whether or not they felt that you should or should not entertain a relationship with someone who is perhaps not as strong or rooted spiritually as you are. They all said, "No!" I believe that this is a valid question and point. Looking at it realistically, I wondered how many of them answered that question due to religious beliefs or just saying what they thought I wanted to hear. Either way I believe that knowing what you need spiritually again can make or break your relationship. For me, being a preacher, I don't necessarily need another preacher as a mate but what I do need is a supporter of my ministry. Yes, I do want someone who is saved, but they do not have to be "limelight Christians" as I call it. One who is seeking after God in all honesty is good enough for me.

What is it physically that I want?	While physical appearance is not and should not be a deal breaker, there may be some attributes that are needed for your level of comfort. This goes back to the chapter that we talked about needs and wants.
What are my expectations of my mate?	This question is a loaded one. We are not talking about the superficial list of wants and don't wants, but the heartfelt list that is for your eyes only. What is it that you Realistically expect from your mate from the basic needs to the most complex? After you answer this question with your list, revisit that list and see what are deal breakers and what is it that you can live with.

CHAPTER 5

PERSONAL BELIEFS ABOUT SINGLENESS

This chapter is where my focus group came in and played a huge part in. What I did for this section is I asked a number of "Teach Me How to Live *Realistically* Single Questions of the Day" via social media and I polled a number of singles that I knew and many that just joined the bandwagon later. I gathered their answers and interpreted the findings under each question. I intentionally never posted my responses; I saved them for the book.

The way that this section is broken down is there is the questions of day, the results of the findings and my personal response.

1. Question of the Day

Multi-dating-where two people agree to see other people with the understanding that they will not sleep with others, but just chat outside with others until exclusivity is established. What are your thoughts?

Response Overview:

Many people were for the concept of multi-dating, but many who voted to do it, all agreed that communication is a vital part of it all.

My Personal Belief

I can and do go both ways on the topic. I feel, for me, that multi-dating is safest, especially for women. See, we are emotional creatures by nature. If we date or talk to one guy exclusively, we have a tendency to get attached to them and therefore often walk away hurt because we were not his choice of mate. However, if we also are multi-dating, then our emotions are less likely to get too emotionally involved too soon and it lessens the likelihood that we will get hurt as easily. With that being said, I also think that there should be a timeline to the multi-dating as well as an understanding.

For me, my personal rule is if you leave me on the market more than a specified amount of time, or we go without communicating for an extended amount of time, there is no need to pursue a relationship, we should just move on.

2. Question of the Day

What are some of the biggest regrets of choices that you have made being?

Response Overview

The responses of the day were numerous, but no matter how plentiful they were, they all pretty much fell under these 6 headings: time, feelings, restrictions, none, denial and lack.

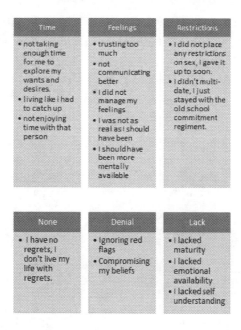

Time	Feelings	Restrictions
• not taking enough time for me to explore my wants and desires. • living like i had to catch up • not enjoying time with that person	• trusting too much • not communicating better • I did not manage my feelings • I was not as real as I should have been • I should have been more mentally available	• I did not place any restrictions on sex, I gave it up to soon. • I didn't multi-date, I just stayed with the old school commitment regiment.

None	Denial	Lack
• I have no regrets, I don't live my life with regrets.	• Ignoring red flags • Compromising my beliefs	• I lacked maturity • I lacked emotional availability • I lacked self understanding

My Personal Belief

My personal beliefs as far as regrets is the fact that first and foremost, we all have some whether you want to admit them or not. We all have some things that we wish we could have done differently or maybe not have done all together. My regret is the action of losing myself in the parameters of a relationship. You know that point where you get so far deep into it that when it's over you have to take the time to remember what you liked, and what you wanted, and your desires for your life.

Another regret that I have is not knowing or recognizing my own strength. I stayed longer than I should have, loved harder than they did, and stayed loyal to a fault only to wind up hurt anyway at the end.

3. Question of the Day

What are 3 things that you wish someone would have taught you about being single?

Response Overview

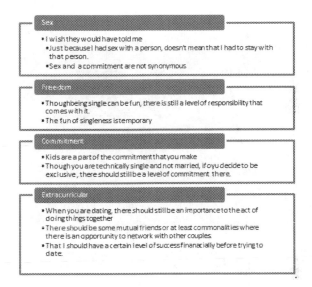

My Personal Belief

There is so much that I wished that someone would have taught me about being single in addition to the points of others.

- I wish that would have taught me how to be single and enjoy it and not feel like I need someone else to complete and/or validate me.
- I wish they would have taught me how to multi-date so that I could have experienced fewer heartbreaks.
- I wish they would have taught me everything that is in this book so that I could have lived a more successful and productive single life.

4. Question of the Day

What are the pros and cons of multi-dating?

Response Overview

Pros	Cons
• *Realistic* expectation with no emotional attachments	• It is harder to create an emotional attachment
• free meals and the beginning of a friendship	• none
• Schedule is too busy for such activity	• It can and will be a headache
	• Schedule too busy for such activity

My Personal Belief

Pros

* Less chance for emotional attachment
* You don't wast time
* You are less likely to miss an opportunity for true love

Cons

* You lessen the likelihood that you can attain an emotional attachment
* You increase your chances of wasting time.
* You could possible lose the opportunity of meeting THE RIGHT ONE while talking to THE WRONG ONE

As you can see, I am tied on the matter because for every positive, I can counteract it with one negative. I do believe that every case is different, so one should proceed with this dating method with caution.

5. Question of the Day

What are flame killers for you in your relationship?

Response Overview

- *Hygiene*
- *Dishonesty*
- *Inability to effectively communicate (both too much and not enough)*
- *Jealousy*
- *Being ignored, disrespected and disrespected*
- *Confrontation*
- *Lack of affection*
- *No follow through on commitments*

My Personal Belief

I entitled a whole chapter "flame killers" in this book, but in short I also completely agree with all of the issues that the panel mentioned.

6. Question of the Day

Do you have or refer to a list of desires and demands when dating? Do you think they are important or Realistic?

Response Overview

The votes are in

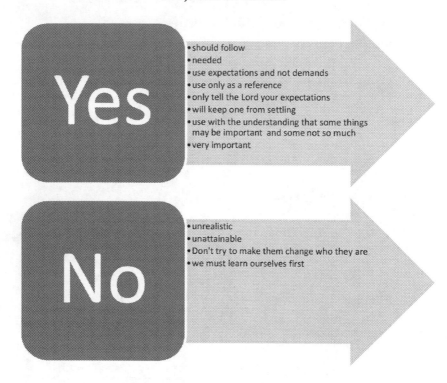

Yes
- should follow
- needed
- use expectations and not demands
- use only as a reference
- only tell the Lord your expectations
- will keep one from settling
- use with the understanding that some things may be important and some not so much
- very important

No
- unrealistic
- unattainable
- Don't try to make them change who they are
- we must learn ourselves first

<u>My Personal Belief</u>

While I do believe that a list can play an important role in the processes of dating for all of the reasons stated

above, I also think that we need to be *Realistic* in our approach and use of it. Using it as a reference is a good idea, but using it as a checklist can and oftentimes will make one miss the mark on their blessing.

<u>7. Question of the Day</u>

What are the greatest lessons you learned from prior relationships that you won't do again?

72

Response Overview

- *Don't remain involved in one sided relationship*
- *Don't tell everything about me*
- *No longer accept less than what I give*
- *I don't have to settle*
- *Can't fix nor change them*
- *Compromise too much/lost myself*
- *Allow God to control the relationship*
- *Never let another person take away their manhood/womanhood*
- *Never hurt someone you love*
- *Don't be so clingy*
- *Communicate more*
- *Don't cheat*

My Personal Belief

This was a very profound question with a lot of different responses, but majority of them all dealt with the losing of one's self in the pursuit of a relationship. This is my personal regret as well. We talked a lot about this in the self-solidarity chapter of the book under "Safety".

8. Question of the Day:

Do you find it easier or harder to get with or find your place in the life that has already attained or is attaining their life goals and dreams or to get with someone who is headed in that direction?

Response Overview

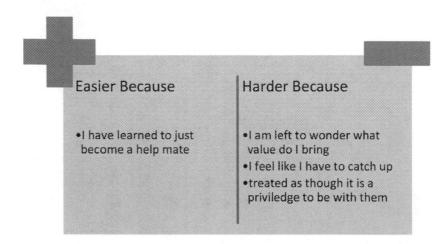

Easier Because	Harder Because
•I have learned to just become a help mate	•I am left to wonder what value do I bring •I feel like I have to catch up •treated as though it is a priviledge to be with them

> ❖ *Depends on the attitude of that person is what many said which means that they don't necessarily find it easier or harder but equally challenging.*

My Personal Belief

This question really sort of hits home for me because I am often the one more established party in my relationships. I also fall prey to some preconceived notions or assumptions that people have about people like me. Ideas such as

- ➢ She's probably arrogant...NOT!!!
- ➢ She's probably a player...NOT!!!
- ➢ She probably doesn't know how to treat a man...NOT!!!
- ➢ She probably wants someone with accomplishments equivalent to hers...NOT!!!

These are just a few of the assumptions that people make about me when the truth of the matter is that these things couldn't be more wrong. I am more often accused of being too nice and the most humble person you could ever meet. I am definitely not a player because I know how it feels to be on the other end of the spectrum. I definitely know how to treat a man and in no way do I want a man with equivalent accomplishments but I do want someone who has something to bring to the table though. My advice is to get to know the individual that you are interested in no matter their accomplishments or lack thereof.

9. Question of the Day

Do you feel it important to share your list of expectations and desires with your potential mate or use it as a resource for your eyes only?

Response Overview

A complete tie amongst the panel

My Personal Belief

I am tied on this question as well and here is why;

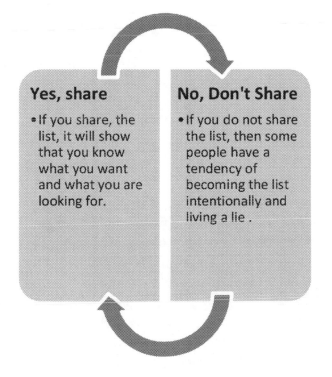

Yes, share

• If you share, the list, it will show that you know what you want and what you are looking for.

No, Don't Share

• If you do not share the list, then some people have a tendency of becoming the list intentionally and living a lie .

10. Question of the Day

Should you tell your mate everything about you at the onset of the relationship or no?

Response Overview

With this question, to my surprise, most of the team said no, you should not tell them everything and they all had valid reasons for their responses.

The theme of the yes responses were along the lines that if you do tell them all, it will empower them to make an informed decision as to whether or not you are what they want for their life. Others wanted to just let the past be the past and move forward. Many say it shows that you have nothing to hide.

For the no group, they were thinking along the lines of telling too much may make you seem over anxious which could lead you to possibly scaring them away. Some say oftentimes, the information is used against you in some way later down the line; some went as far as to say that you will hear it in divorce court.

My Personal Belief

This one is a tough one for me because I do believe in establishing lines of open communication and honesty. With that being said, what I do is I listen to the general conversation to hear for certain things that they may have an issue with such as women preaching, homosexuality, and the like. When we encounter such subjects, I then let it be known that I fall or used to fall in that category. This allows them to make a decision as to whether or not they want to still proceed or not. As far as them using it later, that is when I remind them, yes, that WAS or IS me and I told you that to empower you to make the decision that you made so therefore, here we are. Most of the time that shuts the mouth of the lion and I keep it moving.

11. Question of the Day

Is jealousy in your mate a positive or a negative?

Response Overview

The panel all agreed that a little jealousy in your mate is cute and makes one feel validated but on the other side of the coin…too much jealousy can be dangerous especially if coupled with possessiveness.

My Personal Belief

I do believe that this issue is a two edge sword that can be harmful especially in certain types of relationships. For instance, in the line of work that I do, where I am considered a public figure, there is no room for jealousy because I am always taking pictures and showing affection to fans so a jealous mate can be a career killer for me.

12. Question of the Day

When multi-dating, should there be an agreement on parameters for the relationship and when you know when to pursue a relationship or to just let it go?

Response Overview

YES!

My Personal Belief

As with any relationship and any topic, there is a conversation that has to take place as to how long the multi-dating should occur. With this in mind, the understanding is established that there are two risks that you take if this goes on too long.

- You could lose a potential mate
- Someone else could take a potential problem off of your hands.

This is another dichotomy of multi-dating. There has to be parameters to the time frame simply because the point of dating is to secure a mate and not continue in the dating pool.

13. Question of the Day

If you have ended a relationship and the individual comes back, would you give a second chance or no and why?

Response Overview

The group was in sync on this topic as well. Most of them said that depending on the situations that they would. Variables such as witness of growth would be needed; forgiveness on both ends would be needed, as well as a reevaluation of the end of the relationship.

My Personal Belief

I personally beg to differ. I have done this before in days gone by, but the lesson that I learned is that it often repeats the same ending. Yes, I do believe that it depends on the relationship, but for me personally, I just steer clear of decisions like that. I call it, "driving in reverse."

14. Question of the Day

What are some pros and cons to rekindling a former relationship?

Response Overview

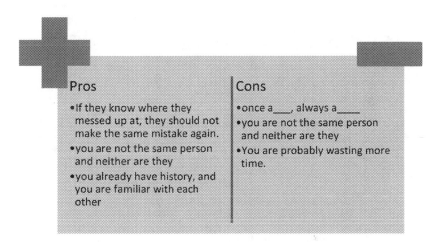

Pros
- If they know where they messed up at, they should not make the same mistake again.
- you are not the same person and neither are they
- you already have history, and you are familiar with each other

Cons
- once a____, always a____
- you are not the same person and neither are they
- You are probably wasting more time.

My Personal Belief

Again, I concur with the panel, however, I am leaning more towards the cons, as I stated it prior questions, I just choose not to drive in reverse.

15. Question of the Day

When dating, do you feel the need to have a set of mutual friends to double date with, hang out with and the like?

Response Overview

The panel came back tied on this topic. They believe that going on double dates and having mutual friends will allow one to observe their potential mate in a group to see if they cast judgment. Some even pointed out that the two can serve as an example of what should happen in a relationship but more so it allows the couple to experience some diversity amongst their friends. Though they were split down the middle, they all agreed that it is not a need but it does have its benefits which are many.

My Personal Belief

Though I agree with the panel, I have a bit more insight into it. I think that as a couple they should have other couples to hang out with for several reasons;

- There should be times for double dates and mutual friends to break the monotony of being just the two of you all the time.
- This also allows you time to network, so to speak, and to see if there are commonalities between the couples, both good and bad and how issues were overcome and how victories were celebrated.
- I believe in my "wanna" and "don't wanna" lists and sometimes being out with other couples, you can add to both sides concerning your relationship and how you want it or don't want it to be.

With this all being said, I believe that there has to be a balance with the couples stuff. There has to be the ability to be separated as a couple as well as alone, down time individually. These balances allow time for reflection and appreciation of each other and the relationship and yes, even the friendship.

16. Question of the Day

Do you think that a person should achieve a certain level of success financially before trying to date?

Response Overview

To my surprise, this was another one that was tied down the middle with more leaning towards the "no" answer.

My Personal Belief

This question runs pretty deep for me because of my status, I do believe that everyone should have something to bring to the table. Even in your pursuit of your dreams, you should currently have some assets to present. Meeting halfway is always best so that one does not feel a certain way financially and succumb to the pressure of feeling needed or wanted for any other reason than love.

17. Question of the Day

What is the biggest deal breaker in a relationship?

Response Overview

For this question I took the top three of what society says are deal breakers which are cheating, finances, and communication. They rated them in importance in the same order; first was cheating, then finances and last was communication.

My Personal Belief

On this issue, though it was a poll, I expected a different result. I guess because I feel so strongly about communication ruling the nation that I felt that others did too. Though I abhor cheating, especially since I have been on both ends of that hurtful spectrum, I still think that communication should have been first in line. I am one that because I am so busy, communication is vital to me. I will leave someone if I don't hear from them daily. I am not saying that we have to eat, sleep, and breathe on the phone but touching base throughout the day is key to me. If that can't happen, I don't want it and as far as finances, it goes back to everyone being on the same page and having something to contribute to the relationship and the household.

18. Question of the Day

What are some cautions that you would warn people about with online dating?

The general consensus of this question is covered in the past online dating section but here are the major takeaways;

Red flags are;

- Check them out by matching what they say with what they wrote.
- Find a rule of thumb for you and follow it. Mine is the rules of three. Three caught lies and I am done and those lies can be by commission or omission.
- Always run a background check if it gets serious.
- In all interactions use caution, don't share too much too soon especially when it comes to personal information like phones numbers and addresses.
- If there is someone who only can text and never talk, you may have to question their motive.
- If there is someone who can only talk before or after a certain time, you may have to question their motive.

These are just a few of the points that you may want to take into consideration with online dating. The number of red flags that one takes is completely a personal preference. For me, there are no more than three, before I cut communication.

19. Question of the Day

What are pros and cons of online dating?

General Consensus

Pros	Cons
Easy to meet people	Dangerous
You may meet people you would never otherwise meet which diversifies your horizons	Be cautious of the lies

Again, we did a whole chapter for online dating that you should visit often if you are considering it.

20. Question of the Day

What are methods or ways that you use to meet people?

Response Overview

YES	NO
ONLINE	**CHURCH**
Enables an opportunity for diversity	I say no to this because it is not my focus during worship, also if it goes wrong, you are left feeling awkward which defeats the point of worship.
COMMUNITY EVENTS	**WORK**
It shows a clear common interest	This should go without saying, but it is a true conflict of interest and can lead to professional destruction.
DAY TO DAY LIFE	**PROTECTED CLASS EVENTS (I.E. JAILS, PRISONS, SHELTERS ETC.)**
It just happens much easier	These people are in a place of recovery and personal healing and discovery and to entertain a relationship may only hinder the process.
	CLUBS
	I just have a personal belief that where you find them is where you will leave them.

My Personal Belief

As much as we may want the traditional grocery store, gas station, and church or community meet and greets, times have changed tremendously. There are many more unconventional ways of meeting people. While I agree with the panel on their modes of meeting others, I would like to take that a step further and make recommendations of where to and NOT TO meet people.

Am I saying that my no places and ways are absolute? No! There are always exceptions to the rule, I just want to present some cautions for you to think of as you entertain the idea of where you choose to meet people.

21. Question of the Day

When dating, what do you think is on the minds of individuals when they post their profiles? Are they true to who they are or do you think that they are saying what "they believe" you, as the opposite sex" want to hear?

Response Overview

The general consensus was to just be honest and true about who you are and what you want, there may be someone who wants someone like you. If you just want a cuddy buddy (Sex mate only), someone may just take you up on that because they are looking for the same.

My Personal Belief

I am thoroughly convinced that people do a little of both. They tell you a little about themselves, play it safe about certain questions like having children or desiring to have children and even their professions and possessions, but all of that goes back to what they think you want to hear.

One that comes to mind is that they love the Lord, which may be true, but men always assume that saying stuff like they enjoy walks in the park, holding hands, walks on the beach at sunset and crap like that gets them brownie points but this is not always the case. With that being said, there are people who say that on their online profiles that they say certain things or leave out certain things for the sake of conversation and I do allow a little room for that but then I seek clarity on the things that they did say in addition to that.

22. Question of the Day

Do you have a personal timeline that you take when one relationship ends and when you begin another one?

Response Overview

Most think tankers said no and some said that they have waited as long as two years.

My Personal Belief

I personally believe that there is a timeline, but the length of that timeline varies and can be dependent on a few things like;

- ➢ **The length of the relationship**
  - o *The longer that you were in a relationship, the more time you may need to heal and get them out of your system.*
- ➢ **The depth of the relationship**
  - o It doesn't take as long to get over a relationship that you were not deep into versus one that you had invested everything into.
- ➢ **The type of relationship (abusive or no, heterosexual or homosexual)**

o   If you have found yourself in abusive relationships, there definitely needs to be a time of healing and restoration for you versus if you weren't. Also if you were in a homosexual relationship, especially if it was your first one, you may need some time to rediscover your desires and see which way you want to go. This takes deep time of prayer and meditation to accomplish and honest reflection.

23. Question of the Day

If a man and a woman each have their own place and they decide to marry or cohabitate, who should give up their place?

Response Overview

90% said to find a mutual place

10% said the man should give up his place

My Personal Belief

Being a woman, I have always been the primary breadwinner of my household. I have always had my mate to come and live with me and my children out of convenience. With that being said, now in my older age and the fact that I am an empty nester, I agree with the think tank on this one. I do believe that "AFTER MARRIAGE" a couple should find a mutual location to reside. I have a home that is designed for me only in mind and I am seeking a mate who has the same so to ask us to readjust our lives in that manner of making room, I would rather just seek out a new mutual spot that we can accommodate both of our tastes, needs and desires and therefore there is also an invested interest.

24. Question of the Day

Many have a tendency to lose themselves during the life of the relationship for lack of balance. What are ways to avoid that?

Response Overview

The general consensus is finding a balance between selfishness and selflessness.

My Personal Belief

I believe that my beloved think tankers hit the nail on the head for this one. Now I want to extend their thoughts on this one and talk about ways not avoiding this pitfall.

How to Balance Selfishness vs. Selflessness

Dedicate a daily activity for yourself

- *This can be something as simple as journaling to exercising but one thing a day must be done for yourself, with yourself, by yourself.*

Establish from the beginning that there has to be some self-time

- *This plays into the teaching people how to treat you and the expectations that you have for yourself as well as your relationship.*

Never give more time to others than you take for yourself.

- *Remember you have to have a reserve for you before you can meet the needs of others, otherwise, you wind up in personal overdraft.*

EPILOGUE

Now that we have finished the reading, now it's time to have a little fun. Enclosed in this next section is a workbook that is more of a card game. As with any standard deck of cards there are 52 cards with various conversation starters for the sapiosexual, inquisitive, curious single. This is a preview of my "*Realistically* Speaking" card game. These questions can be used as a reference when seeking to start a conversation or just to get to know each other. Many of them come from the book and some are just general questions. How ever you want to use them is up to you but as with all of my books I always seek to enclose some sort of interaction and this "workbook is the interaction for this project. There are many ways that you can use them.

- Cut the pages out, cut the cards out and use them as a regular card
- You can use them as a resource within the book and you and your potential mate can answer them on paper (separately) or make a date night out of it with a relaxing environment.
- I make a game out of it setting a timer for one minute after I ask the question and they have to answer the question before the timer goes off.

However, you want to use it, have fun with it and put it to use. There are also other decks of cards that are even more fun available on my website at jgilbertministries.com

AFTERWORD

Teach Me How to Live *Realistically* Single Workbook

1

How do you feel about multi-dating which is where we will see other people while considering if we will date?

2

What are some of the biggest regrets of choices that you have made being?

3

What are 3 things that you wish someone would have taught you about being single?

4

What are the pros and cons of multi-dating?

5

What are flame killers for you in your relationship?

6

Do you have or refer to a list of desires and demands when dating? Do you think they are important or **Realistic?**

7

What are the greatest lessons you learned from prior relationships that you won't do again?

8

Do you find it easier or harder to get with or find your place in the life who has already attained or is attaining their life goals and dreams or to get with someone who is headed in that directions?

9

Do you feel it important to share your list of expectations and desires with your potential mate or use it as a resource for your eyes only?

10

Should you tell your mate everything about you at the onset of the relationship or no?

11

Is jealousy in your mate a positive or a negative?

12
When multi-dating, should there be an agreement on parameters for the relationship and when you know when to pursue a relationship or to just let it go?

13
If you have ended a relationship and the individual comes back, would you give a second chance or no and why?

14
What are some pros and cons to rekindling a former relationship?

15
When dating, do you feel the need to have a set of mutual friends to double date with, hang out with and the like?

16
Do you think that a person should achieve a certain level of success financially before trying to date?

17

What is the biggest deal breaker in a relationship?

18
What are some cautions that you would warn people about with online dating?

19
What are pros and cons of online dating?

20
What are methods or ways that you use to meet people?

21
When dating, what do you think is on the minds of individuals when they post their profiles. Are they true to who they are or do you think that they are saying what "they believe" you, as the opposite sex" want to hear?

22
Many have a tendency to lose themselves during the life of the relationship for lack of balance. What are ways to avoid that?

23
If a man and a woman each have their own place and they decide to marry or cohabitate, who should give up their place?

24
Do you have a personal timeline that you take when one relationship ends and when you begin another one?

25
Do you have/want children? How is your relationship with the mother?

26
Have you ever been married? How many times? Will you do it again?

27
Where do you want to live/retire?

28

Do you
smoke?

Do you
drink?

29

Describe your
personality in
one word?

30

What is it that
you are
looking for in a
mate?

32

What is your
intent for
dating?

33

What was
your longest
relationship
and what
happened?

34

How do you feel
about pets?

Do you have
any?

And what are
they?

35

How
ambitious are
you about
life?

36

What are
your hobbies?

37

What are
your goals
and
aspirations?

38

What makes
you unique?

39

What kind of
music do you
like?

40

What is your
religious
preference?

41

What are your educational experiences?

42

How do you feel about sex before marriage?

43

How do you feel about living together before marriage?

44

What are your plans after retirement?

45

Where are the places that you desire to go but have never been?

46

Do you consider yourself a neat freak or a messy bessy?

47

What are your musical preferences?

48

What do you do for fun?

49

What do you do to relax?

50

What is the advice that you would give to your younger self?

51

How do you feel about cheating?

Is there a prevention for such action?

52

How important is_____to you?

(You fill in the blank)

CONCLUSION

I hope that you have enjoyed this literary experience. Again, I am sure that I am not telling you anything you don't know, but my desire is to give you something to think about as you partake in the single lifestyle. Remember that there is a consequence for every action that you take and you have to be mindful of what you do knowing that your future is impacted. I did not come to tell you to or not to have sex. I didn't come to tell you to or not to live together prior to marriage, nor go against any religious beliefs or personal convictions that you may have but again just to empower you with knowledge to make good, sound, wholesome decisions.

I don't consider myself an expert at living single, but I have made my share of mistakes and have learned from them. I have also watched the mistakes made by others and learned from them as well. I consider myself the vessel that God uses to convey information to the masses. I make myself available and he pours into me what needs to be said. So I hope that something was said or done to empower you to make better decisions.

RESOURCES

<u>Emma Thornett</u> wrote the great article referenced in this text entitled, "Satan's lies about singleness" I encourage you all to read it because it truly blessed my life.

<u>http://matthiasmedia.com/briefing/2013/08/satans-lies-about-singleness/</u>

Bible verses came from <u>https://www.biblegateway.com/versions/</u> where there are a plethora of versions of the bible that you can use to help you understand scripture We used the King James version for the enclosed scriptures.

ABOUT THE AUTHOR

Dr. Jennifer Gilbert, Ph.D

Dr. Jennifer Gilbert is a mother of two adult children and a grandmother to one beautiful grandson. She has written books for every walk of life to include Christianity and Education. This is her first single's self-help book, but demand says this won't be her last. Through her "Teach Me How to Live Realistically Single" Think Tank Group a number of married and single people have flocked to her weekly live Facebook chats to get her divine revelation of the lifestyle we call "singleness".

After two failed marriages, and a season of sexual preference confusion, Dr. Gilbert gathered the members of her being, rededicated her life to Christ holistically, and began a life of celibacy in await for her mate.

Through her single's work she has found her own self to be more empowered to live a better life as a single, celibate, professional woman. Her charge to all singles is to live a life of forward thinking accountability. Looking forward to how today's decisions will affect tomorrow's relationships.

Teach Me How to Live Realistically Single is just the beginning of that work. She has also created her own card game line for singles to occupy them with fun, date night activities to divert the attention away from inappropriate and premature energies that could lead one to regret.